# Debt Free Forever
### BY J.J. JONES

*The Ultimate Guide to "Knowing Nothing to Having Everything in Financial Freedom, Becoming a Millionaire, and Becoming Debt Free Forever"*

**Debt Free Forever 2<sup>nd</sup> Edition**

**Copyright 2014 by J.J. Jones - All rights reserved.**

In no way is it legal to reproduce, duplicate, or transmit any part of this document in either electronic means or in printed format. Recording of this publication is strictly prohibited and any storage of this document is not allowed unless with written permission from the publisher. All rights reserved.

Debt Free Forever 2nd Edition

# Table of Contents

Introduction ..................................................................... 4

Chapter 1: Why and How Deep are You in Debt? ................. 5

Chapter 2: Income vs. Expenses ......................................... 9

Chapter 3: Viable Alternatives ......................................... 14

Chapter 4: Common Pitfalls (Get Rich Quick Schemes) .... 19

Chapter 5: Develop Financial Discipline in your Household ..................................................................... 21

Chapter 6: Concentrate on Increasing Income ................. 24

Chapter 7: Keep at It ....................................................... 27

Chapter 8: Paying off your debt one by one ..................... 30

Chapter 9: Financial Education and Business Planning .... 34

Chapter 10: Setting your Financial Goals ......................... 40

Chapter 11: Building your Wealth .................................... 43

Conclusion ..................................................................... 48

Check Out My Other Books ............................................. 49

Debt Free Forever 2nd Edition

# Introduction

I want to thank you and congratulate you for purchasing the book, Debt Free Forever The Ultimate Guide to "Knowing Nothing to Having Everything in Financial Freedom, Becoming a Millionaire, and Becoming Debt Free Forever".

This book contains proven steps and strategies to get you out of debt, help you stay out of debt, and then lead you to financial stability.

This three step process is essential. This is because, much like anything else you do in life, you should not stop at the halfway point. And that is what getting out of debt really is! The other part of being debt free is to become financially stable, so much so that you can live a fulfilling life, afford an adequate lifestyle, and be free from the limitations that your current financial status, shackles you in!

To be perfectly up front, there is no secret formula that is too good to be true. All there is to becoming debt free is knowing what has worked for hundreds of debt ridden consumers. Learning to tweak what works to fully fit your situation. Then, following through with your personalized debt free road map. And making sure you do not repeat the mistakes of your debt ridden past!

Thanks again for purchasing this book, I hope you enjoy it!

# Chapter 1: Why and How Deep are You in Debt?

Before you can determine what type of plan will work for you, first you need to determine the reasons you got into debt in the first place. Be absolutely honest with yourself here! This is because, the efficacy of the plan you utilize, is determined by the accuracy and truth of your assessment. Tip: take your time when making the assessment. Dig deep, and add notes to your list of debts, i.e. was it a failed endeavor, a home foreclosure, a foolish spur of the moment splurge, or a necessary expense like hospitalization fee, did you lose your job, etc.

## Debt Free Journal

At this point, you want to dedicate a notebook, journal, or electronic file for your entire journey. This way you know where you are starting from. You can constantly monitor where you are at. And, you fix your eye on that debt free goal.

You should first set your writing time in your schedule. The best time to do this is in the morning after waking up and doing your morning routine. You could also do it in the evening if this is when you are less productive. Writing in your debt journal is the type of task that is important but not urgent. It is essential to schedule this task because it is easy to neglect. At the beginning of your debt journal, you should write down your debt from different sources.

You should also take note of the strategies that you plan to use to deal with your debt. Every time you implement a strategy, you should take note of it and how it worked out. You should also include the challenges that you commonly face when implementing your strategies and how you overcome them. You should go back to what you wrote every time you feel frustrated by the enormity of your debt.

Keep track of your credit score every step of the way

Aside from the amount of your debt and the strategies that you plan to use, you should also take note of your credit score at the start of your journey. There state-regulated services that will help you get out of debt. There are also a lot of strategies that you can do on your own. You should be aware however, the effects of the strategies and the services that you use to your credit score. For instance, the Consumer Credit Counseling Services are very helpful in giving advice on the best strategies that you can use. However, the use of these types of services can be seen in your credit history and this may affect your credit interest rates in future loans. You should weigh the pros and cons of using any new strategy or service before you fully implement them.

## Accumulated Debt?

How long did it take you to get to this low point? This realization can help you better assess, the reason for your financial woes. For example: you started incurring debt as soon as you lost your job. You tried to make ends meet with a part time job, and kept up appearances by charging heavily on your credit card.

Being aware of the reasons why you accumulated such a large debt will help you deal with it. Most people tend to deal with debt problems with quick fixes like not going out as much or taking additional jobs. Regardless of how much you save and earn however, you will not be able to pay off your debt if you don't deal with the deeper reasons that caused your debt in the first place.

How does your mind react to temptation?

Many people who get into debt have bad financial habits. They either spend too much than what they earn or earn too little for their needs.

Those who earn too little need to find other sources of income that will help them earn more money. People, who are in this category, often create excuses why taking a higher paying job is not a good idea. They often don't want to leave their current job because they have a fear of leaving their comfort zone. You'll know if you are in this category if you earn less than most of the people around you.

Those who spend too much have a problem with giving in to temptations. Whenever they see something that they like, they immediately justify the purchase as they take the item and move towards the cashier. People in this situation often have too much purchased items at home or are subscribed to services that they know they cannot afford.

You need to know if you have any of these habits that are keeping you in debt. If so, you will need to overcome them and replace them with more productive habits. If you are a shopaholic for example, you can easily avoid over-shopping by avoiding places where you may get an urge to buy something that you don't need. On the other hand, if you are a procrastinator and it prevents you from getting a promotion at work, you need to motivate yourself to keep working and avoid distractions that prevent you from doing your best.

## How Much Exactly?

List down "ALL" your debts. It would help a lot if you could list them down from the most interest accruing, oldest debt, biggest single debt amount, etc. Make sure to have a separate sum for: due and demandable debts; about to be due (1 month or less), future collectibles, etc. Tip: if you know how to use Microsoft Excel, or any similar computer program, this should make your life a lot easier!

## 30% Rule

If you take 30% of your monthly income (assuming you have income), How long will it take for you to pay for all your debts? This should provide you with a rough estimate. Of course, if you have disposable, liquid assets, then the timeframe should be accelerated.

## Chapter 2: Income vs. Expenses

An income vs. expense worksheet is necessary for you to determine how much of your income are you spending. You can utilize your I&E worksheet in several ways. This includes but is not limited to:

- Knowing how much you actually spend vis a vis how much of that spending you can cut off.
- Knowing how much income you still need
- Pinpointing the area where you spend the most and then determining whether or not it coincides with your priorities.

Common sense says that you can spend as much as you make in a month. But common sense is not very practical. That is, if you want to get out of debt and eventually earn millions.

### 30% Surplus

In reality, it is a good idea to save up at least 20% to 30% of your monthly net income. Leave that untouched and deposit it in your savings account for a rainy day! Anything below 20% and you are overspending way beyond your means, or you are not earning enough income.

### Sources of Income

"ALL" sources of income must be considered. From your salary, income on rental property, interest income, etc.

### What Income to Include?

If you are the sole provider for the household, then you include your total net income. This is gross income minus taxes. If you have another member of the household who fully shares his/her income to the household i.e. spouse, then add their net income as well.

If another member of the family shares only part of their income, then only add that to the total net income. Make sure to only include regular contributions. For example:

Mr. A 2,000 net monthly

Mrs. A 1,500 net monthly

Son A 300 monthly contribution

## Total Expenses

For accurate results it would be best if you had receipts for your expenses. Tip: if you enroll certain accounts online, then you have easy access to your tabulated expenses i.e. Credit cards.

## Miscellaneous Expenses

Make sure to include all expenditures. For example: miscellaneous expenses that you might have overlooked. This includes paper money you had to exchange or buy gum or buy bottled water with, for spare coins you need. You then whittle away at your expenses until you only have spare change for unnecessaries and 99% of your spending is fully identifiable.

Tip: any money you can't account for, when balancing your income and expenses goes to miscellaneous. This way you actually see how much of a sinkhole your unnecessary expenses are.

## Savings Account

You need to deposit that 30%, preferably more of your income on a bank account. This gets credited to your list of expenses. This way you are creating a good credit standing with your bank, to offset, at least to a certain extent, other declared debts you might have. Perform a general cleaning in your home and collect all your spare and unnecessary change. Deposit these as well!

## Tightening the Belt

Look at your income and expense worksheet. Try to remove anything or minimize any and every area in your spending. For example:

Minimize takeout and start cooking meals. Minimize meat purchases and balance it out with fruits and veggies. Stop buying fizzy and sugary drinks. All you really need is water. In this regard, tap water is usually safe for drinking! Bottled water really is unnecessary! Also:

- Gas expense can be minimized by commuting once in a while. Walking or using your bike when doing small errands also helps.
- Do you really need that new cellular postpaid plan? Why not keep your old phone, minimize calls by texting, and consolidating your internet plan.
- Do you really need cable TV? Most of the things you watch anyway you can get online!

## Things You Can't Skimp On

Regular home maintenance, auto insurance, tuition fees, taxes, regular medical checkups, etc. are things you cannot skimp on! Pay these on time and in full!

For example: Real estate insurance or other one time payments per annum must be factored into your expenses, divided into as many months, as the next installment. So if you still have 6 months to go, you can divide it in 6 monthly expense cycles. Never utilize your savings account for this. Your savings account is only to be used to pay debts and for emergencies.

**Talk to Your Debtor**

The last thing you want is to forget about the debt. The best thing to do is to talk to your creditor and ask for an extension. Even if this is not possible, keeping lines open can save you lots of troubles in the near future.

**Freeze Interest Rates**

If your creditor is a private person, maybe you can ask for an extension, without payment of interest. Explain your situation fully.

If your debtor is a bank or lending institution, there may be a grace period clause you can use. Although, be absolutely sure about using the grace period since this is most likely a onetime deal.

**Switching debts**

You can also ask if some demandable debts can be converted into a loan, i.e. A credit card debt converted to a personal bank loan. The interest rate is usually lower and you get to pay installments.

**Mortgages**

If you have a mortgage then you need to start thinking of how important that mortgage is to you and your capacity to pay. Your rule of thumb is to keep only what you can pay for and prioritize your needs.

For example

A family home is important, but if you cannot really afford the home then, maybe it's better to let go while you're able to. Do you really need that automobile? Remember you need to factor in amortizations, gas, upkeep, insurance, etc. If you can go to and from work via commute, then, maybe letting go of that car is the right thing to do.

If you have spare properties, then it is best to let go of the same to pay for debts. I.e. A second home, second automobile, expensive jewelry, etc.

But you need to learn when to let go and when to hang on to your properties. A good rule of thumb is to factor in interest payments and penalties. Then determine if lowering the asking price will allow you to save money or not.

To be perfectly honest, if you can pay your debts by selling peripheral or spare properties, then do it! But if selling your property only cuts less than 50% of your debts, then you need to look for other alternatives first.

## Chapter 3: Viable Alternatives

Let us assume that you looked into your income and expense worksheet, you looked into your savings account, and you even factored in your real and personal properties. You've also contacted your relatives. But you are still short of paying "ALL" your debts. You need a little bit of help from a third party. Below are a few financial tools that you can utilize.

### Real/Personal Property Mortgage

If you don't want to sell your property outright, you can mortgage it. Some authors will even tell you that taking out a second or third mortgage are alternatives. This author is of the opinion that you should NOT take out a second or third mortgage.

As a general rule, you stick to 1 mortgage per property. This is because; in most cases it will result in you making your debts more complicated! Best case scenario, you delay the demand ability of the debt. Worst case scenario, you lose another property, you get buried in more debt, more interest payments, and more penalties.

When mortgaging a property, always sign a deal on the winning side. This means you know you can handle the amortizations. You know you can keep the property. You know you can pay your debts in full.

### Refinance

A refinance is a secondary mortgage that takes the place of the old mortgage. This can be from the same lender or different lender. A refinance is a viable alternative for those who are in a better position to renegotiate their loan terms. This includes, but is not limited to:

- A better credit report and score
- A better economy
- Promotional refinance rates
- A substantial down payment you've saved up
- You qualify for government mandated/regulated repayment plans

## Fixed Rate All the Way

A caveat, you always want to know how much you will pay on the loan from the first amortization to the last amortization! So, whenever you apply for any loan or refinance your loan, it is almost always a good idea to make sure that your interest payments are fixed. Yes, there are a couple of exemptions wherein you can opt for adjustable rate mortgages and/or balloon payments, but these are very rare cases.

## Debt Consolidation

Debt consolidation is a viable alternative for debtors who get confused by the many debts they have. Think about it, isn't it easier to pay just 1 loan with one interest rate and due once every month; as opposed to several loans, due on different dates, with different interest rates, from different lenders.

Aside from being convenient, lumping all your loans into one, may also afford you the advantage of a lower total interest rate. This means, the sum total of all your interest earning debts minus all your debtors, is higher, than the interest rate offered by a single lender.

It is always a good idea to consolidate "ALL" debts into one. But in some cases, you can leave out a couple of debts from the loan. It really is up to you and the advantages you can get form the consolidation.

## No Longer Due

When you consolidate a loan, due debts become future debts. The total loan amount is divided into as many installments you and your lender agreed to. So you get a little bit of breathing room for at least a month.

## More Onerous

Take note however, that one big debt is more destructive to your credit score, especially if it is a consolidation loan. This is not really a threat if you will be paying on time and in full. But if you default, then literally trouble begins to occur. Pay special attention to an acceleration clause. And at the very least, default in one consolidation loan and other lenders will be hesitant to provide you another one.

Simply put, this alternative is viable for a consumer who is in debt partly because of negligence, lack of skill in budgeting, and who might have experienced a temporary hardship in his/her finances.

## Bankruptcy

There are several types of bankruptcy filing. This article will discuss the 2 most common types of private individuals, as debtors. Bear in mind that bankruptcy is not a magic pill. Not everyone is allowed to take it and not everyone will get "better" because of it. But if taken by the right consumer with proper planning and due execution, it can save you from overwhelming debt.

## Means Test

This test initially determines what type of bankruptcy you can file for, or if you can file for one to begin with. The BK court will then assess the filer to determine if the BK will be allowed to prosper or should be dismissed.

## Credit Rating and BK

There are a lot of "so called" experts who tell you that BK will ruin your credit report. News, flash, the fact that you are already buried in debt also ruins your BK. Yes your filing will make your credit score drop some more, but chances are, it will drop to that same low, even lower, if you keep bleeding due and demandable debts. Think of BK as an amputation of a limb. If you don't amputate, you'll die due to blood lost and or infection. The only plus side to a BK, is whatever you lose, you can eventually get back!

Yes, BK will last for 7 to 10 years depending on the type of BK and the length of the repayment plan. Within that same timeframe your facility of credit will be limited.

## Lawyer of Self filing?

In theory, a person can file for BK without the help of a professional and/or lawyer. The forms and instructions are available for free via Bankruptcy courts, or online. In reality, only those with limited assets, "ALL" within the same state can realistically file for BK "pro se" (by themselves) i.e. a house, a car, some cash, etc. If you have several properties, some of which are out of state, then you need to at least hire professional and state licensed BK filers or lawyers.

## Automatic Stay?

An automatic stay means creditors who do not hold a security over your property, cannot go after you, while your Bankruptcy filing is being heard by the BK court. Do not believe everything you hear. Yes, a BK filing can allow you to stop a bank from executing/foreclosing on your property, but only for the time being. This is because a bank or creditor has a mortgage or security clause that the BK court must respect. The best it can do is stay foreclosed for a couple of months. All the creditor does is file a petition in court showing a better right, then they can continue with the foreclosure.

## Chapter 7

Also known as liquidation BK. As a general rule, any property not declared as exempt and not requested to be excluded is included in the BK filing. Chapter 7 is most applicable for those who have overwhelming debt, and have no capacity to pay.

Exceptions both as to type and amount depend on the state where you live. At the very least, a modest family home, unattached by any independent creditor can be exempted. So are modest clothing, furniture, professional articles, limited cash, etc.

## Chapter 13

This is also known as repayment BK. The filer/debtor has financial capacity, but inability to pay the full amount of all debts. The creditors do not want to negotiate so the court steps in. Usually this involves cutting off the interest payments and penalties from all debts. Repayment usually lasts a couple to several years. While you are under repayment you need to pay on time and in full, lest your creditors find a hole they can exploit!

# Chapter 4: Common Pitfalls (Get Rich Quick Schemes)

When trying to get out of debt, you need the right type of information, the right type of remedy, the proper plan of attack and a steady hand to follow thru until the last payment. The problem is, there are so many ways you can get things wrong. Below are a few things to steer clear of.

## Who to Listen to

You don't want to listen to any Tom, Dick, or Harry. You want someone who has been there and done that! The author of this eBook is one such person. He started off as a debtor, crippled by credit card debts, a car loan, and a home mortgage. He was literally crawling form one paycheck to another. It took a while but eventually, all debts were paid.

## Too Good to be True

It probably is! There is no easy way to get out of debt, especially substantial debt. You really need to tighten your belt and rack your brains. There is: no secret formula, no secret technique your creditors don't want you to know, no single tip that is so effective it should be illegal. Stay the course of paying your debts!

## The Road You Take

Getting a refinance when in fact you know you are stretching things is a bad idea. Filing for BK when you can actually pay, will lead to a dismissal of your case. Tightening your budget when it is already so tight you are living a miserable life is also a bad idea. There are several financial tools you can utilize to get out of debt. Find that proper tool and utilize it!

Tip: consult with a credit counselor. The same counselor you will need a certificate from to file for BK. These individuals are state licensed and are neutral third parties. They can advice you on your viable alternatives based on your personal and financial situation.

**Payday Loans**

Simply put, payday lending is a bad idea. The interest rate is off the charts, and the ability to get instant cash is addictive to some individuals. And you have better alternatives. Chances are you still have a credit card, why not use that instead. But only in cases of emergencies!

**Service Providers**

You either buy a book to know what to do or hire the services of someone who will do everything for you. You don't buy a book with a service at a bloated cost, so someone can talk to you over the phone and "guide" you thru your problems. Heck, better call a credit counselor!

# Chapter 5: Develop Financial Discipline in your Household

The people you live with are also important in your quest to get rid of all your debts. If you have a family, the big chunk of your income is most likely being spent to provide your dependents with their needs. One of the reasons why parents get into debt is because they've been providing their children with the kind of lifestyle that they cannot afford. As stated in the previous chapters, you need to control your monthly spending to 70% of your income. It is impossible for you to follow this budget if your kids keep asking more than you can afford.

## Tell everyone about your financial goal

To make sure that everybody cooperates with your goal to get out of debt and to build wealth, you should let your family know of the true financial situation. You should take time to gather your family members, tell them about your debt and how you plan to deal with them. You will get different types of reactions based on the personalities of your family members. The only exceptions here are family members with psychological problems and children who are still too young to understand.

If this task is not possible in your position, you could only limit the people that you tell to those who are able to help in the situation. The sooner you tell everyone about it, the easier it will be for you to live within 70% of your current income.

Telling other people in your household about your concern will put everyone on the same page. They will understand why you have to limit your spending compared to what you spent before. It will be easier to convince children and teens to lessen their spending. This could also serve as a motivating factor for some of the members in your family to save up and be more responsible with their money.

If you spend a lot of time with friends, you also need to tell them about your financial goal. There may be times when you need to avoid the temptation of going out with them. To avoid feelings from getting hurt, you need to tell your friends that you are in a mission to get out of debt and ultimately improve your financial situation. If this doesn't work, you could tell them of a more concrete goal like saving up for a house or a car. People are more understanding if they know your struggles.

## Implement your plan together

After telling everyone about your current dilemma and the plan you've developed using this book, you should then start implementing the plan in your everyday expenses in the household. Instead of using more than one car for example, you could car pool with your family members to work and to school. This will help you limit the amount of gas consumed and it will also help everyone get to their morning destinations on time. You should also consider buying cheaper brands that you are not used to buying especially if the product performance is just the same.

Instead of expensive dinners in high-end restaurants, you could enjoy your bonding times at home. Quality time with your family doesn't have to be expensive. Vacations are not off-limits as long as they are within your budget. One way of reinforcing money-saving behavior in kids for example, is by telling them that they have a reward if they keep doing positive behaviors. You could then reward them with fun activities like going to the beach or the park.

You should also limit consumption in some areas of household spending. For instance, if you have more than one TV at home, you could only use the best one and leave the other ones off. This way, you will be able to spend entertainment time with the family while lowering power bills. You could also take out old board games and teach your child how to play it. By doing this, you diversify your child's experience in having fun.

## Use money as a reward

If you have children in the house, developing a saving mindset will also be helpful as they grow up. If they develop the right money management skills at a young age, they will be able to avoid debt when they start earning. To develop these skills, you need to give your child a budget and teach him or her about setting financial goals, saving and even working more to earn more money. The principle that you impart to your child will help him in understanding why there are times when you need to save money and not spend on all the things that he wants.

## Develop your own money management skills

The skills that you will learn from this book are only the beginning. Money management skills are not taught in school except if you major in personal finance. To learn how to manage your money effectively, you should read more on similar topics. The principles that you learn of your readings should then be practiced and taught to the people that you live with. The people in your household will only follow what you preach if they see you practice it.

# Chapter 6: Concentrate on Increasing Income

As mentioned earlier, you can only tighten the belt so much! You need to realize that you are budgeting to streamline your spending and to instill a discipline in yourself. When money is still short, and most probably it will be, then an additional source of income is the better alternative. Below are a few ideas.

**Ask for a Salary Increase**

If you come on time, rarely get absent, have excellent performance, then a raise is in order. Most companies have an assessment every 6 months to 2 years. When is your next assessment? Prepare for it! And make sure your company does provide for a salary increase.

**Get a New Job**

You'd be surprised that most debtors are employed. The problem is, they are under employed or are working on a dead end job. Here is a good rule of thumb. If you have been working for the same company for 3 years with no salary increase, with very little to do, and nothing important to contribute, then better get out! You want a job where you matter! Where you are part of the decision making! Where a salary increase for good performance is a sure thing!

**Part Time Job**

While you are looking for your dream job, you might as well augment your income by getting a part time job. The trend nowadays is to get an online job. This way you can go home, be with your kids, and still sneak in a couple of hours of work. If you are the man/woman of the house, then an online job allows you to add to your household's income, while still being able to take care of the kids or your elderly parents. Pick an online job that fits your skill and interest. You have dozens of options: transcription, teaching, back office documentation, auditing, content writing, website design and/or maintenance, marketing.

To make time for your online job, you should organize your schedule and look for areas where you can have some alone time in front of your home computer. During this time, tell everybody around the house not to disturb you. After that, you should make a list of your skills that you can offer to online clients. Your most important skills are the ones that you have most experience in.

You should then look into online job sources and create your accounts. There are multiple gurus online who write and make videos on how you can make your professional profile look appealing to possible employers. These profiles will serve as online ads for your personal services.

After that, you should then start preparing for online interviews. These interviews usually take place online through online video calls like Skype or Google hangout. You will need to dress up for the occasion in your professional attire and start practicing to answer basic questions that are usually asked in your industry. If you are hired, you will need to clarify your working time and develop a system that will allow you to be fully awake in your working hours. If you are working for foreign clients, there may be a need to work at night to adjust to their time zone. In this case, you should find another schedule for sleeping.

## Build relationships with your clients

In the online job marketplace, you are competing with people from all around the globe to win jobs. Most of these jobs are offered to people from developing countries because they can be paid less. To make sure that you always have a job ready, you should build a good relationship with your bosses. You could do this by doing excellent work all the time. You should also make sure that you communicate well with your boss through email. For project based jobs, don't hesitate to ask for more opportunities when the project ends. People who do online business also have connections in the same industry who might hire you. They will only refer you to their connections if they are satisfied with your work.

## A Caveat

You are looking for an online job to make money, not part with your money! So steer clear of multi level marketing schemes, membership schemes, forex, bitcoin, stocks, etc. Simply put, anything that requires you to pay money first to get money is a no-no. No matter how tempting the offer is!

## Don't spend more as your income increases

It is common for people who have increased their income because of a part-time or second job to also increase their spending in miscellaneous expenses. Some think that because they are working so hard, they are entitled to more pleasurable purchases. If you are still in debt, you should not allow yourself to fall in the same trap. You should still stick to our 30% rule even when you are earning more money than ever.

# Chapter 7: Keep at It

Admit it, you are reading this eBook, thinking to yourself "This is easy, I can do that!" Yes you can! But several months into your well thought out plan, you start to cheat, with one credit card charge here, a new flagship android or Mac phone there, a designer pair of jeans here, and you're back to racking up debts!

Go back to your journal! Remember how bad things got! Don't let that happen again. You need to get to zero debt before making a substantial purchase! Heck, a smart phone can last you 3 to 5 years before it conks out. You're old jalopy can last even longer. Clothes, you can occasionally buy some, but only non signature brands and timed during big sale dates. You can splurge from time to time with food. This way you don't feel deprived, but only within reason and within budget!

## Go Easy on the Credit Card

You do not need to cut your credit cards. At least, not unless you have more than three. Keep the most useful and oldest cards. Not necessarily the ones with the highest credit limit. Only use it for groceries, gas, and important purchases. Make use of the convenient points that you get.

## Get an Anti-Debt Buddy

If worse comes to worst and you can't follow through with your planning, you should find someone who will help motivate you manage your debt repayment. Ideally, this should be someone that you live with. This person will remind why you should not be spending more than 70% of your income. This should be a person that you respect and that is concerned for your wellbeing.

The plan is set and all you have to do is to implement it. However, implementing your plan is not easy especially if you are trying to unlearn a lifetime's worth of bad financial habits. Your buddy will act as your primary motivator. He understands you and what you are going through and he knows the things that motivate you. He functions similarly to a trainer in the gym. He will be there when you are struggling to deal with temptations and when you are frustrated when trying to make ends meet.

**Motivate yourself everyday**

Zig Ziglar, a motivational speaker, once said that motivation, like taking a bath, should be done daily. You will need a lot of discipline to be able to deal with your debt. To keep your discipline high, you should try to re-motivate yourself every day. Make a list of the stimuli that motivated you in the past and use them on a daily basis.

Your aim is to motivate yourself to earn more and spend less. To do this, you need 2 types of motivation; a motivation routine and an emergency protocol for urgent motivation improvement.

Your motivation routine, as the name suggests, is a group of tasks that you do regularly to improve your motivation. For instance, you could meditate every morning after arriving to your office to develop mindfulness early. You could also read motivational literature online or in physical publications. Other people are motivated by their children. If you are too, you should spend some time to bond with your kids before work and school. These simple tasks will remind you why you need to earn more and spend less every day.

There are also times when your mood changes abruptly. This could happen because of a bad day at work or unexpected expenses like sickness or something needs to be fixed around the house. These mood changes can shift your motivation from being enthusiastic to being frustrated. This is when you will need a quick motivator to increase your enthusiasm. If you are easily motivated, playing your favorite song will be enough. However, if this doesn't work for you, you could take some time to realign your focus towards your goals. If you are religious person, you could meditate or pray.

## Record your performance

Money management is not rocket science. It can be done with simple math. You should have a clear idea of the amounts that enter and come out of your pocket. If you are a fan of any sport, you may be motivated to decrease your monthly expenses and increase your income by recording your performance. Most athletes keep themselves motivated by trying to beat their personal best records. You could also keep track of your records using your journal. Every time you earn and spend, you should keep your personal record in mind and try to beat it.

## Celebrate Milestones

Every month you successfully stick to your plan, order a box of pizza, or celebrate with a reasonably priced bottle of wine. Anything to tide you over for the long haul! This should keep your spirit up until you become debt free.

# Chapter 8: Paying Off Your Debt One by One

You will need a lot of diligence to pay your debts on the shortest time possible. To make sure that you don't spend the money that you should be using to pay your debt, you should create a system that will decrease your exposure to the spending temptations.

### Look for automatic payment options

If you successfully consolidate your debt to one loan, there are some financial institutions that will just deduct that amount you need to pay as soon as your payday comes. This system will make debt payment automatic and it will relieve you of the burden of resisting temptation. You will also notice that it is easier to stick to your budget using this system. Because you don't have extra cash in your bank account, you will not be able to deviate from the plan that you created.

If you were not able to consolidate all your debt into one loan, you will need to develop a system of paying off some debts first. To do this, you need to go back to your list of debts. If you haven't done it yet, you should arrange the list according to their interest rates. The ones with the highest interest rates should be on top of the list.

### Prioritize debts with higher interest

When paying off multiple debts, you should deal with the ones on top of your lists first. They are the ones that will grow faster and they will become impossible to pay if you neglect them. If you have 3 debts from multiple sources for example, with the following rates:

Debt 1: 50,000 at 6% interest rate

Debt 2: 40,000 at 3% interest rate

Debt 3: 80,000 at 1% interest rate

Most people would think that it is wise to pay off the debt that has the highest amount. In our example, the debt with the highest amount is currently $80,000 with an interest rate of 1%. This means that every month, your debt will increase by $800. On the other hand, the debt with the highest interest rate currently amounts to $50,000 at 6% interest rate. If you don't pay this off soon, this debt will grow by $3,000 every month. Though you should not neglect any of your debts, you need to divert your paying power to the debt that grows faster. If you take home $6,000 every month, 30% of that should be $1,800.  You could allocate $1,000 dollars to the one with the highest interest, $500 to the one with second highest interest and 300$ to the last one. When one of the debts is gone, you could now increase the amount that you pay according to the interest rates of the other two. Make sure that you always pay above the minimum required. This habit will keep you ahead of the interest rates.

## Or pay off the debt with the smallest amount first

There are some people who prefer to see results as soon as possible. If you are this type of person, the "snowball method" of paying your debts may work better for you. In this method, you arrange your debts in a list from the smallest amount to the largest. When your payday comes, you pay all the debts with the minimum amount except the smallest one. You pay this particular debt with the rest of the 30% of your income. You will eliminate this debt after paying a few times. When one debt is eliminated, most people become motivated to deal with the next one. You should do the same strategy by transferring most of the payment to the next smallest debt.

### Transfer debt from one credit card to another

There are some credit card companies that allow you to transfer your balance from other credit cards. If you still haven't reached the limit of one of your cards and it has a smaller interest rate, you could use this option. There are also some credit cards that offer a zero-interest transfer. You should consult the bank or credit card representative for the advantages and risks of using this option. These types of promos usually allow you to transfer your debt to another company and let it stay there for a period of time without interest. Some banks allow you to keep your debt for 12 months while there are those that allow longer periods of up to 18 months. The zero interest only lasts for that period. If you still have debt after this period, the bank will now increase your interest rate to their standard rate. You should consider this transfer if you will be able to pay off the debt that you transferred before the zero-interest transfer period expires.

### Throw all your bonuses to paying your debts

Many people are so excited to spend their bonuses. You are not entitled to spend any extra income as long as you have debt. Consider your bonuses a tool to increase the rate of reaching your goal. Because you are comfortable with spending 70% of your usual salary for your lifestyle expenses, you can use the whole bonus that you receive to pay off your debt.

### Look for money hidden away

Look into all your savings accounts and see if you have anymore that you can spend on your debt. You can start depositing to your savings again when you are debt-free but for now, your priority is to stop the bleeding by taking care of your debts as soon as possible. You could also check if you and your spouse have any amount in your life insurance policies' cash value. You could withdraw these amounts and use it to minimize your debt growth.

## Borrow money from family and friends

If you have a good reputation with the people close to you, you could borrow money from them and use it to pay off your debt. Debts from social circles usually do not have interest rates. When borrowing, present to them a plan on how you will pay them back. Most people would rather file for bankruptcy than ask for help. If you have children however, you need all the help that you can get to improve your credit rating. If you file for bankruptcy, your rating will take a blow. If you have relatives who will allow you to borrow money, you may likewise entertain this option.

Minimize your expenses

It is common for most people in debt to still maintain their lifestyle because of the social pressures. For a lot of us, keeping up appearances is a bigger priority than actually paying off debt. You should avoid this kind of attitude and focus more on your goals.

# Chapter 9: Financial Education and Business Planning

Knowing how to handle your finances is a tricky endeavor. Sure you can do it by yourself, but it will be a trial and error thing. You have no time for that. While paying off your debts, look for worthwhile seminars. Nope, none of that universe crap! Get something more practical like accounting 101, consumer tax laws and how to use them to your advantage, or tax shielding, etc.

**The Ultimate Goal**

Remember, you want to be a millionaire, after you pay off your debts. How do you expect to handle that kind of money without proper schooling! At the very least, your financial education can provide you necessary certifications and contacts if and when you set up your own business!

**Why Put Up a Business?**

Your goal is to be a millionaire! The fastest way to that goal is thru your own business! So, what are you good at, what is your passion, what are you educated for? Remember that savings account? Aside from using that for your debt payments, you can also use that to put up a modest business.

**Learn about the business that you want to start**

Starting a business can be frustrating if you don't know what you are doing. Many businesses fail because people begin their start-up without gathering enough information. You should make sure that you know all that you need to know about the industry that you are getting into to avoid wasting your hard earned money on failed ventures.

There are various ways that you can learn how to start a business properly. One way is to observe the systems developed by other businesses and taking note of how you can apply them. Look for a similar business in your area and take note of important details like their sources of products and the amount of employees that they have. Aside from that, you could also read about the type of business that you are about to get into. Books are easiest to obtain now through online shopping sources. Lastly, you can ask advice from a person who has succeeded in a business type that you want to start. Many successful people will give you valuable advice for free. Some people that you can ask are your boss and industry leaders that you meet in seminars and conventions.

## Start with a hobby

You can also get more business ideas by looking into the things that you enjoy doing. Many of the greatest entrepreneurs of our time were hobbyists before they started out making business. Steve Jobs and Steve Wosniak were really interested in computers before they decided to create a business out of it. Nick Woodman, the founder of the sports camera company GoPro, is a surfer and it is during a surfing trip when he was inspired to develop a camera that can be mounted to sports equipment.

Look into your interests and your hobbies for inspiration for products and services that you can provide. You don't have to create a new product to build a successful business. Most of the time, all you need to do is to look for sources of products that aren't available in your area of operation.

## Setting aside money for your business

Though you can start a business with very little cost, your options will be limited if you don't have sufficient capital.

When you've paid off your debt to half, you should already start saving up for your business goal. If you can save another 5% from the 70% that you spend from your income, you will be able to accumulate some funds that can be used for starting a business. You can do this while you are still learning about the new venture. By the time you are ready to start your business, you will have some funds to use for your start up.

### Develop a business plan

Consider setting up a business like any other big project. In any project, preparation is crucial. Using the information that you've learned, you should start creating a business plan. You should include the products or services that you want to sell. You should also add the sources where you will get the products and services that you want to provide to your customers. You should also consider your location. Do you need a physical store or do you focus on your online presence?

The most important part of a business plan is the capitalization and the projection of your business' return on investment. Simply put, how much do you need to spend to start your business and make it survive and how are you going to profit? When the answers to these questions are crystal clear to you, then you are ready to start building your business.

### Social Media Helps

Nowadays, a physical store location is no longer necessary. Put up shop at home. Make sure you have the appropriate certificates. Potential customers can visit you in a homey looking nook. Get some professional looking pictures. Don't pay someone; chances are you have a relative who has a professional grade camera! Now advertise online. Tap your family, relatives, friends, etc. Now use their social network to increase your coverage. Remember, your goal is to set up shop with minimal capital outlay. Most of your funds should be used for your goods, or inventory!

Tip: put up a dedicated page for your business. Link social media outlets like Facebook, twitter, Instagram, SalesForce, LinkedIn etc.

You should choose the social networking website where your target market can be found. For instance, LinkedIn users are all professionals. If you have a product or service that caters to the needs of millennial professionals, you should maximize your use of this website. Both twitter and facebook have a lot of millennial users however, twitter users click more on ads and twitted promotions than facebook users. Before deciding to spend a lot of time to build a social media focused business, you should first learn about the differences of each website and which one will work best for your products or services.

## Selling excess items from around the house

The simplest business that you can put up is a garage sale. Because of the popularity of the social media, you can also sell items that you no longer need online. People have been doing this in classified ads websites for more than a decade now. With the amount of time that people spend in social media, you can now reach more prospect buyers without leaving your home.

To start your selling business, you need to look for items that will fill your inventory. Make sure that you no longer need these items and that they can still be used by other people. You should also make sure that they are still presentable. People who buy online usually depend on the photos to help them decide to make a purchase. If the items that you are about to sell do not look good on photo, they will not sell.

## Simple Value

All you need is a product that meets a certain human need. It has to be cheaper, do things better, or in a different way than your competition. Now run with it! Try a viral ad campaign on YouTube, Instagram, tweeter, etc. now set up several ads, and see what works and what does not.

## Price Wars?

If you don't have a unique product, or if there are other sellers who have a different version of your product, the last thing you want is to cut prices to try and undermine the competition. This can lead to a price war that is bad for business. What you should do is try to carve your own following. Remember, with the social media generation it's all about lifestyle and branding.

## Go Local First

Identify your product or service with your locality. Again use social media to carve out a local following. This should set you apart from out of town and state sellers/services. Personally interact with buyers. This increases your support and the information you get can be useful in version 2 of your product and/or service.

## Focus on niche markets

In any product that you sell, chances are good that there are other people selling similar items. If you are competing with a long established store brand, you will not last long because people prefer to buy from places and brands that they are familiar with. To make your business prosper even when there are a lot of competitions, you should target a niche from your overall market and cater to their specific needs.

A niche market is a smaller part of the industry market that is made up of people who have similar unique needs. Let's take the camera industry for example. There are already a lot of well established camera manufacturing companies before GoPro released its products. The people behind GoPro knew that they will have no chance of competing against big brands. The main edge of their products is its usefulness to active people and athletes. Their target buyers are the entire population of camera users around the country. However, they chose not to advertise their products to the whole populations of buyers but instead focus on the sporty niche of the market. You should also do the same when selling your products and services. You should provide added value that will appeal to the niche that you plan to sell to.

## Go to Conventions

Visit conventions showcasing your business. Get ideas from them! See if you can widen your product or service base with some of the ideas and contacts you get from that convention. Your next step is to put up shop in a convention hall.

# Chapter 10: Setting your Financial Goals

There are a lot of people who want to become successful but do not really know what success really means. Your quest for success is like a journey. You can never be successful if you do not set a clear destination for your journey. In our quest to get out of debt and achieve financial freedom, we should set a financial goal that will guide our actions.

### Creating your life goal

All the successful people you know have one thing in common; they know what they want and they work every day to get it. You should also take some time to step back from your busy schedule and start thinking of what you want to achieve in life. The average person has between 70-90 years before they expire. Chances are good that you've already spent at least 18 years of your time here on earth. Now, you need to decide what you want to achieve with the time that you have left.

What do you want to buy in the next ten years? What school do you want your children to go to for college? How do you and your partner want to spend your retirement?

These are only some of the commonly asked questions when people plan their life goals. If you examine any of those questions, you will see that your ability to reach those goals is intertwined with your financial situation in life. It will be impossible for you to reach most of the goals that you set if you are in debt.

### Planning your activity based on your goals

Because you are reading this book, your first financial goal should be to pay off all your debts. To do this, you need to make sure that you maximize the amount of money that you can earn with your time.

The amount of money that you will gain on a regular basis will depend on how you exchange your time. Your daily activities can be converted into money. This is what experts refer to as active income. The principles in this book taught you to use 30% of your income for paying off your debt. If your income is low, that amount will also be low and it will take you more time to pay off your debt. The only way to reach your first goal faster is to increase your active income.

There are two types of active income. The first one is your regular income which includes your salary and the other monetary rewards that you get for being an employee. The second type is commission income which is only received when the right outcomes are achieved. For people who work in sales, this is the type of income that they are used to. Employees also get a similar type of income when they receive performance bonuses.

To reach your first financial goal faster, you need to have these two types of active income. You should keep your day job. If you don't have one, you should look for one. After establishing your schedule in your day job, you need to look for a second opportunity where you can get commission income as a sideline. Your salary will ensure that you receive a regular amount every month. Your commission-based job on the other hand, will allow you to increase your income based on your activity on your free time.

Having these two jobs will increase your income and it will make sure that you will be busy working all the time. You should spend the time when you are not working with your family or the people you are close to. Because you are busy at work and with your family, you will no longer have time to shop, dine out with friends and do other things that promote spending.

Your second financial goal

After you've paid off your debts, it's time for you to change your financial goals. The habits and the discipline that you've developed in reaching your first one will help you reach this goal faster. The nature of this goal is to increase your wealth. However, declaring that you want $1,000,000 million dollars will not really help your motivation. For you to become truly motivated to achieve a financial goal, you need to associate the numbers with what you're going to use it for. For instance, you may say that you want to buy a house or a car. You could also say that you want to use the money to send your children to a good college. Your financial goal should be extremely important to you so that it will motivate you to work harder and to sacrifice today's pleasures so you and your family can live a better life tomorrow.

## Make your goals more specific

For your goals to truly guide your daily actions, you need to make sure that they are clear and cannot be interpreted in any other way. For instance, saying that you want to "pay off your debt" will not be very effective in guiding your actions. In this example, you need to add how much debt you need to pay off and the amount of time needed to pay it off. The time that you allot yourself should be both challenging and realistic. You need to challenge yourself to pay your debt off as soon as possible.

Now that you have a vague idea of what your two most important financial goals are, you should use the money principles discussed in this book to create a plan that will help you reach them.

# Chapter 11: Building your Wealth

The skills and principles that you learned in the previous chapters should not be forgotten. You should keep practicing them even though you've become debt free. On the day that you already have zero debt, you are not completely out of the woods yet. This is the time when you should start building your wealth.

Continue to increase your income

For you to become prosperous, you should continue to increase your income by improving your productivity at work. If you continue to increase the value that you add to your company, the people in charge will soon take notice. Always keep your attention on the next promotion.

You should also continue to keep your eyes open for new opportunities. Keep working hard on your part-time job and try to enjoy working. The income sources that you developed when paying your debt will be useful when you are saving up for the business that you want.

**Spend less than you earn**

Even though you don't have debt anymore, you should still continue to spend only 70% of what you earn. However, you can now use the remaining 30% to start developing wealth for the future of your family and for yourself. Just like when you were still paying off your debt, you should allocate the 30% first every time you receive money on payday. You could save them in a bank account or invest in an investment tool.

**Start making your money work for you**

Think of each dollar you earn as a servant who can work for you. If you spend them on consumer products, you are exchanging your servants for products. If you want to be able to live comfortably in the future, you should set aside your servants for future use. While you're not using them, you should not allow them to be idle. This is why you need to start investing. When you invest, you are making your servants work to obtain more servants.

Many people fear investing their money. However, if you plan to be truly rich without spending all your life working, you need to take part in the growth of the economy.

## Replenish what you've lost in paying off your debt

There is a good chance that you depleted your savings accounts and other rainy day funds in paying off your debt. As soon as you finish paying, you should start saving to replenish these accounts. You should first save up for your emergency fund. You should also protect your family's future by starting or continuing a life insurance policy. You should also look into investment linked insurance policies that allow your money to grow faster than inflation over time.

## Start as early as possible

The younger you start investing, the better. However, because you need to deal with your debt first, you are not able to start as early as you would like. As soon as you have paid off your debts, you can now start thinking of investment tools that will help you reach future financial goals. People who start investing early have more time to increase their capital and to recover from economic ups and downs.

## Stick to investment tools that you know

In all types of investments, you should first learn the ropes before jumping in. As mentioned in the previous chapters, there will be a lot of the so-called financial products that will be presented to you as investments. However, you should stick with the big companies when starting to build your investment portfolio as a beginner. When investing, you are basically making the company borrow money. In return, the company gives you part of the ownership in the form of stocks or shares. You make money when the company that you invested in profits and increases the value of their shares. To make sure that you are doing the right decision when choosing the companies to invest in, you should make sure that you stick to companies that you are familiar with.

## Don't follow the hype

Many people are talked into investing into new companies that they are not familiar with because of the promise of great returns. When investing, you should always remember that the amounts of returns and risks are directly proportional. If an investment offers great potential returns, the risks are also high. As the risk decreases, the potential returns also decrease. Most small companies that you haven't heard of that are said to have high potential returns also pose high risks to your capital. This is the reason why, you should only stick to the companies that you are familiar with.

## Start with the basics

The first types of investment that you should start joining are the ones with the lowest risk and the best returns. In most states, the most profitable investments are the ones offered by the government and places that one works for. For most people, their Individual Retirement Accounts and 401(k) plans are the best option to start building assets. Because the future benefits of these plans are based on how much you and your employer have contributed, increasing your income will also improve your benefits in these types of retirement plans.

## Diversify your investments

When investing, you should keep in mind to never put all your eggs in one basket. This means that you should always diversify your investments whenever possible. When choosing which investments to diversify your money into however, you should choose the investment types that will fit your goal. If your goals are long term, which could range from 10 years of more, you could invest your money in high risk and high returns investments types like mutual funds with equities as the underlying assets.

Financial goals that are shorter than that are considered short term. When investing for these types of goals, you want to minimize the risk to make sure that the capital is preserved. That means that you should park your money in investment tools where there is very little chance of losing it. For beginners, the best types of investments for these kinds of goals are mutual funds with bonds as underlying assets. Mutual funds are an investment tool managed by an investment company. In a mutual fund, the company gathers the money of investors and combines them to one fund. The company's fund managers then invest the money in various types of investment tools to increase the funds value. This type of investment tool is great for beginners because an expert will manage the money for them.

As you learn more you could diversify your money to the stock market. Before you do however, make sure that you have studied and understood the risks involved.

## Learn before you invest

In anything that involves money, it is absolutely necessary to learn first before you invest. Even with your retirement funds for example, you should know where your money is going as you pay them. You should know what the right amount to pay is and what your payment duration will be. You should also become aware of the risks involved in all the investment tools that you take part in.

Most people think that making money is based on luck. They only say this because they do not understand how the system works. Your most important task in your quest to earn your first million dollars is to continue on learning. Observe the people that you look up to and copy the admirable characteristics that they have. With the right balance between discipline and desire, you will gain enough money to reach your financial goals.

## Conclusion

Thank you again for purchasing this book!

I hope this book was able to help you to: realize that there is a way out of overwhelming debt; you need to outfit yourself with the right tools, and execute the right plan; you need to follow thru until you have zero debt; and, you need to step things up a notch and augment your income!

The next step is to go back to your journal. Re-read the eBook to get more insight, add some more notes. Now consult with a debt counselor! Pay the minimal fee, and make sure to get the certificate you need, just in case you need to file for BK in the near future.

Remember, getting out of debt is not a race. It is a marathon that requires mental toughness and endurance. You should pace yourself, don't run out of steam midway thru!

Finally, if you enjoyed this book, please take the time to share your thoughts and post a review on Amazon. We do our best to reach out to readers and provide the best value we can. Your positive review will help us achieve that. It'd be greatly appreciated!

Thank you and good luck!

## Check Out My Other Books

Below you'll find some of my other popular books that are popular on Amazon and Kindle as well. Simply click on the links below to check them out. Alternatively, you can visit my author page on Amazon to see other work done by me.

Marketing Money Mastery

http://amzn.to/1hxUaj6

"Debt Free Forever"

http://amzn.to/1qrgldh

Money Management Makeover

http://amzn.to/1hAU8Z7

Single Women and Budgets

http://amzn.to/WPRJ3M

www.ingramcontent.com/pod-product-compliance
Lightning Source LLC
Chambersburg PA
CBHW071827170526
45167CB00003B/1452